## I. Introduction

Since 1984 antitrust law has shown a growing respect for the threat of entry as a condition to immunize from legal challenge a merger that otherwise would significantly increase the probability of collusion. Yet the economics literature would appear to indicate that a collusive agreement should not fear entry in the presence of positive sunk costs. This suggests that either the courts have a better grasp of economic realities than economists or that the importance of entry conditions in merger analysis is likely to decline in the future as the courts incorporate the latest economic learning into the case law.

In this paper, we attempt to bring theoretical form to a particular entry argument that has found favor in the courts. We suggest that sunk costs may not be a major impediment to entry when a group of customers can commit to an entry enhancing strategy. The simplest example involves a large buyer that is able to guarantee an entrant a market for its product. Long term contracts or even informal purchase commitments (backed by customer reputation) may also allow the entrant to obtain a guarantee of sufficient business to make the entry profitable. Once entry is thought likely to occur, the existing competitors will be unwilling to attempt a price increase. That is, the threat of entry can maintain competitive prices even in the presence of sunk costs.

In Section II, we motivate the analysis by discussing the current controversy over the role entry conditions play in a merger review. Then we discuss the necessary assumptions for a model of the threat of entry in the presence of sunk costs. Section III contains the details of our general sunk cost model. We illustrate how large buyers, uncertainty, the cost of collusion and market growth can interact to maintain competitive pricing. We also discuss how economies of scale can affect the threat of entry. The general applicability of the model is discussed in Section IV with evidence from recent federal court antitrust litigation.

1

## II. Entry In Economics - And Antitrust

Baumol, Panzar, and Willig (1982) show how the threat of entry into a perfectly contestable market can be sufficient to deter price from rising above competitive levels, regardless of the level of concentration in the market. As Schmalansee (1987 at 42) observes, however, the contestable market result may describe an "empty box". In practice, the necessary condition for contestability of zero sunk costs seems unlikely to be met. Without this condition, contestability theory seems to have little to tell us about the threat of entry for antitrust policy.

Consider, for example, a competitive market with a downward sloping demand curve and a few competing firms facing potential entrants with small but positive sunk costs. Should the firms in that market decide to collude and raise price, they have no apparent reason to fear entry. While a prospective entrant may observe prices that would make entry profitable, those prices are, from the point of view of the entrant, merely a mirage. As soon as it enters the market, prices will be driven below the pre-entry competitive level.[1] Thus, the entrant will lose the opportunity to capture profits from supra-competitive prices and at the same time lose money on its sunk costs, even though it has a cost structure identical to the entrenched competitors. Entry in such circumstances would appear illogical. Knowing this, incumbent firms would appear able to raise their prices collusively without the worry of entry. (See, for example, Stiglitz, 1987 at 886 and 890, and Harrington, 1989 at 386-9.)

Despite the fragility of the contestable market result, in recent years courts have been willing to find for defendants in merger cases on grounds of the threat of entry. Starting with *U.S. v. Waste Management*, 743 F.2d 976 (2d Cir. 1984), courts have consistently

---

[1] Given that collusive schemes are inherently unstable, we assume that the disruption of entry breaks up the collusion. The additional output of the new entrant then drives prices below the pre-cartel level. Theoretically, entry increases the returns to cheating on collusion, because it is uncertain to members of the cartel whether they are losing sales to the new entrant or to an incumbent who is cutting price. For discussions of the effects of uncertainty on collusion, see Caves and Porter (1978) and Baker (1989).

found against the government in highly concentrated industries with few or no apparent barriers to entry.[2] Thus, one could conclude that some showing of entry barriers is now a necessary condition for a merger to violate the antitrust laws.

The official government policy on entry written into the Department of Justice (DOJ) Guidelines (1984 at paragraph 3.3) is somewhat unclear, stating both

> If entry into a market is so easy that existing competitors could not succeed in raising price for a significant period of time, the Department is unlikely to challenge mergers in that market.

and

> In assessing the ease of entry into a market, the Department will consider the likelihood and probable magnitude of entry in response to a "small but significant and nontransitory" increase in price.

The Guidelines then define the magnitude of "small but significant" as a five percent price increase (although this figure should be adjusted for special industry conditions) and interpret the time frame for "nontransitory" as generally two years.

The first quote suggests that the DOJ will focus on how entry conditions affect the profitability of a nontransitory price increase. The threat of entry within a two year time period can render a price increase unprofitable, if the expected expansion of output lowers long run price sufficiently to reduce the profits of the colluding firms below the level associated with competitive behavior. This point is implicitly recognized in a footnote to the Guidelines that posits the prospect of entry may have a deterrent effect on the exercise of market power.

---

[2] Other examples include *U.S. v. Calmar Inc.*, 612 F. Supp. 1298 (D.N.J. 1985), *F.T.C. v. Promondes*, 1989-2 Trade Cas. (CCH) 68,688 (N.D. Ga. April 14, 1989) and *U.S. v. Country Lake Foods, Inc.*, No. 3-90-101, (D. Minn. June 1, 1990). The courts appear to consider both a time and a cost dimension to entry barriers.

The second quote highlights more tangible affects of entry. By focusing on the likelihood and magnitude of entry, the Guidelines suggest that it is the magnitude of entry that will occur during a two year period that should be considered. As entry becomes more likely to eliminate an anticompetitive price increase within two years, the DOJ becomes less likely to challenge the merger.

The two analyses illustrate different approaches to the entry question. The first approach relies on data that suggest that the threat of entry would deter a price increase, while the second suggests sufficient entry should occur in two years to return the market to competitive equilibrium. The first method is compatible with the classical microeconomic theory of markets in which profits attract entry. In contrast, the second approach appears to consider the idea that sunk costs may prevent entrants from investing in a market in response to supracompetitive prices, because the entry could cause the supranormal returns to disappear.

In a recent merger challenge, the DOJ advanced a restrictive reading of this paragraph, arguing that the only way to defeat a presumption of an anticompetitive effect based on high concentration is "by a clear showing that entry into the market by competitors would be quick and effective." Judge Clarence Thomas, writing for the Court of Appeals for the District of Columbia Circuit, rejected the government's approach, concluding that it is unrealistic to expect such strong proof in the context of a merger case and even if a firm never enters a market, the threat of entry can stimulate competition.[3] Thus, although the economic literature appears to support a strong rule for ease of entry as a defense argument, courts appear unwilling to budge from more lax standard established during the 1980's.

---

[3] *U. S. v. Baker Hughes*, 731 F. Supp. 3 (D.D.C. 1990), aff'd. 908 F.2d 981 (D.C. Cir., 1990). In his decision (at 984), Judge Thomas pointed out that "[s]ection 7 [of the Clayton Act] involves *probabilities*, not certainties or possibilities" (emphasis original).

Our purpose here is to present a model that shows circumstances when the threat of entry can deter such a price rise in the presence of sunk costs. We note that a model of entry in this context should have several features. First, it should have positive sunk costs. Second, the model must have a competitive equilibrium with more than one firm. Previous models in the literature, such as Gelman and Salop (1983) and Scheffman and Spiller (1987) have assumed an industry with constant cost curves and positive sunk costs. In such an industry, Bertrand competition generates marginal cost pricing and firms are unable to recoup their sunk costs. Thus, the first firm in the market will remain a monopolist or some form of competition will occur until only one firm remains. Either case is of no interest in merger policy, which implicitly assumes the existence of at least some competition in equilibrium.

Third, entry should threaten to impose positive costs on the colluding firms. If entry reduces incumbent returns back to their previous level of zero economic profits, they will have little to lose by colluding. They will choose to collude, taking the chance of gaining positive profits and the "risk" of zero profits, rather than face the certitude of gaining zero profits. Thus, entry must pose a risk to incumbents' quasi-rents to have a chance at deterring a price increase.

Fourth, it is important to model buyers as strategic players. As Sexton and Sexton (1987) and Scheffman and Spiller (1987) point out, buyers can take actions to protect themselves from anti-competitive prices.[4] In particular, as Demsetz (1968) and Yu (1981) suggest, they can use long-term contracts (of various forms, including complete vertical

---

[4] Sexton and Sexton model a cooperative under certainty and conclude limit pricing is the likely outcome, while Scheffman and Spiller model a market with a large buyer where the supplier must invest in customer-specific sunk costs. They also find limit pricing can occur.

integration, the ultimate long-term contract) to induce entry.[5] What we are presenting here can be thought of as a generalization of Demsetz' original model.

Finally, a model of entry should take account of uncertainty in the market, as has become common in the industrial organization literature over the past decade. The collusive firms are unlikely to know how high they can price without inducing entry. One thing, however, is known for certain: that the potential entrant has not entered. This puts a floor on the costs of entry.

## III. An Entry Game

### A. Rules of the Game

We present a simple one period entry game where the threat of entry can deter, at least under some conditions, any collusive price increase. There are N identically sized producers in this industry, each producing with the same commonly available and known marginal cost structure. Each of the incumbent producers has already paid the sunk costs necessary to enter the industry. To create the required quasi-rents, we assume that the available technology generates for each firm an upward sloping supply curve. This allows for a competitive equilibrium in the presence of sunk costs, and places those firms' profits at risk in case of entry.

For ease of presentation, following on Scheffman and Spiller (1987), buyers have a perfectly inelastic demand for the industry's product. Buyers, however, are allowed to use contracts to induce entry.[6] The lowest cost potential entrant faces some sunk costs $S^E$, the

---

[5] This argument is similar to one used by the Supreme Court in *Standard Oil v. U.S.* 337 U.S. 306-7 (1949), cited in *Sewell Plastics Inc. v. Coca Cola Co.* 720 F. Supp. 1219 (1989). The court stated that contracts are "of particular advantage to a newcomer to the field to whom it is important to know what capital expenditures are justified [because they] offer the possibility of a predictable market."

[6] Conceptually, suppliers could also use contracts to facilitate entry. See the discussion of *U. S. v. Syufy Enterprises*, below in Section IV.

distribution of which we will discuss below. Once the entrant has incurred the necessary sunk costs, it produces with the same marginal cost schedule as incumbents.

In the first stage of this game, producers decide what price they will charge. We assume that they are able to effectively agree on some price to be charged, absent entry, at some cost C. We initially assume C=0.

In the second stage buyers have a choice. They can either accept the industry price or induce entry. Entry is induced by payments from a coalition of buyers.[7] This coalition may take the form of the largest buyer in the industry. Or the coalition may consist of two or more buyers creating a joint venture that produces the relevant product. Or it can take the form of any number of firms entering into contracts with the entrant that compensate the entrant for its losses in a post-entry competitive market. For simplicity, we assume that the transaction costs of forming the relevant coalition are zero.[8] We also assume that entry is induced when there is an arrangement available that is pareto optimal for all members of the buyers' coalition as well as for the potential entrant.[9] The buyer coalition has market share $\lambda$. Once entry occurs, the collusive agreement is assumed to dissolve and firms price at marginal cost.[10]

---

[7] We note that conceptually a buyers' coalition could serve to facilitate of monopsony power. See Jacobson and Dorman (Forthcoming, 1991).

[8] This will be most applicable when the buyer coalition consists solely of the largest relevant buyer. Should there be costs to forming the coalition, those costs should be included on the right hand side of equation (8) below.

[9] In effect, we assume that by offering to pay the potential entrant to enter the market, the buyer coalition can gain information about the entrant's cost structure that is unavailable to incumbents.

[10] This is our equivalent to the "grim trigger strategy" discussed by Harrington (1989 at 388). Such an assumption makes entry less likely because the entrant will not be able to benefit from a "price umbrella" formed by the collusive action.

## B. The Base Case Solution

In the model, demand is perfectly inelastic at $Q$.[11]  $P$ equals price. Incumbent firms price at marginal cost and have supply curve

$$(1) \qquad Q^I(P) = (P-A)/B \qquad\qquad A,B>0.$$

Let $N$ equal the number of equally-sized minimum efficient scale firms in the industry. (Thus $N = 1/MES$, where MES equals minimum efficient scale.) A potential new entrant is willing, after paying its sunk costs, to supply the market with

$$(2) \qquad q^E(P) = (1/N)(P-A)/B.$$

Let $K = N/(N+1)$, $0<K<1$. The total supply curve after entry is

$$(3) \qquad Q^E(P) = (P-A)/KB.$$

Price and industry profits after sunk costs (quasi-rents) before and after entry are

$$(4a) \quad P^I = BQ+A \qquad\qquad (4b)\ \pi^I = Q^2B/2$$

$$(5a) \quad P^E = KBQ+A \qquad\quad (5b)\ \pi^E = Q^2BK/2.$$

Industry profits at least cover sunk costs in the pre-entry equilibrium. The existence of sunk costs insures lumpy entry, which creates the possibility that the existing firms will earn supranormal rents as long as the available returns do not trigger entry. To examine the

---

[11] This is done for the sake of simplicity. Assuming an inelastic demand curve overestimates the return to supra-competitive pricing, the harm to consumers from such pricing, the loss in profits to incumbents due to entry, and the cost to buyers of inducing entry.

entry question, we focus on the profits after entry for the new entrant and all previous incumbents.

(6)    $\pi^E_e = Q^2 K B / 2(N+1)$

(7)    $\pi^E_i = Q^2 K^2 B / 2.$

We know that the potential entrant has not yet entered. We also know from (7) what profits (quasi-rents) it would make, and what the buyer coalition with market share $\lambda$ would be willing to pay it to enter, $\lambda(P^I - P^E)Q$.[12] For this situation to be an equilibrium the amount of sunk costs facing the new entrant cannot be less than the sum of the post-entry quasi-rents and the available buyer payments. Thus, the minimum amount of sunk costs $S_L$ the entrant can face is

(8)    $S_L = \pi^E_e + \lambda(P^I - P^E)Q$

       $= Q^2 K B / 2(N+1) + \lambda(1-K)Q^2 B.$

Since $(1-K) = 1/(1+N) = K/N$

(8a)   $S_L = Q^2 K B[1/2(N+1) + \lambda/N] = Q^2 B K H$, where $H = [1/2(N+1) + \lambda/N].$

$S_M$, the maximum possible amount of sunk costs that the entrant may be facing, remains unknown. Without loss of generality, let $S_M = (1+R)S_L$, $R > 0$, and $S_M - S_L = RS_L.$[13]

---

[12] Note that the larger the market share of the buyer group, the closer the market moves to the contestability result even in the presence of sunk costs.

[13] If the actual sunk costs for the most likely potential entrant were less than $S_L$ then entry will occur and generate a new equilibrium. Then one can repeat the analysis with one more competitor and derive the equilibrium condition.

9

Assume that the cartel raises price above the competitive level by $p_m$. It will be worth an additional $p_m \lambda Q$ to the buyer coalition to induce entry. Similar to Crawford and Sobel (1982 at 1440) and McAfee and McMillan (1987 at 109), we assume that the actual sunk costs of the most favorable entrant $S^E$ are distributed uniformly in the range $[S_L, S_M]$.[14] This implies the probability of entry in response to a price rise $p_m$ is equal to the probability that $S_L + p_m \lambda Q > S^E$, or

(9)    $\text{Prob}(\text{Entry}|p_m, \lambda, S_L, R) = \sigma(p_m) = p_m \lambda Q / RS_L, \qquad 0 \leq p_m \leq RS_L / \lambda Q.$

If the cartel raises price without inducing entry it gains profits

(10) $\pi^C(p_m) = \pi^I + p_m Q.$

The cartel thus maximizes profits over $p_m$, given the probability of entry

(11) $\text{Max } \pi = \sigma(p_m)\pi^E_i + (1-\sigma(p_m))\pi^C(p_m).$

Taking derivatives and setting equal to zero yields

(12) $\lambda Q^3 K^2 B / 2RS_L + Q - 2\lambda p_m Q^2 / RS_L - \lambda Q^3 B / 2RS_L = 0.$

Dividing (12) by Q and rearranging generates

(13) $p_m^* = [RS_L / 2\lambda Q][1 - \lambda(1-K^2)Q^2 B / 2RS_L].$

---

[14] $S_L$ can be interpreted as the minimum estimate of sunk costs in an industry and $S_M$ as the maximum estimate of sunk costs.

Equation (13) implies that the cartel will either limit price, setting $p_m^* > 0$ and face the

threat of entry, or it will not raise price at all. If it chooses not to raise prices, it does so

because the expected profits from $p_m^* > 0$ are less than expected losses from a decline in

price due to new entry. We now assume no price rise ($p_m^* \leq 0$, which implies $p_m^* = 0$ because a

cartel will have no reason to set price below the equilibrium competitive level). Since

$RS_L / 2\lambda Q > 0$, (13) implies

(14)     $2RS_L \leq \lambda(1-K^2)Q^2 B$

$2RQ^2 BKH \leq \lambda(1-K^2)Q^2 B.$

Recall $1-K^2 = (1-K)(1+K) = (K/N)(1+K) = K(2N+1)/N(N+1)$. Simplifying (14) yields

(15)     $2RH = 2R[1/2(N+1) + \lambda/N] \leq \lambda(2N+1)/N(N+1),$

$(2R/[2N(N+1)])/[N+2\lambda(N+1)] \leq \lambda(2N+1)/N(N+1)$

(16)     $R \leq [\lambda(2N+1)/[N+2\lambda(N+1)]].$

Let $N = 5$[15] (MES $= .2$ and $K = 5/6$), $\lambda = .2$ and let $R^c$ denote the critical level of R, above

which supracompetitive pricing will occur. Equation (16) can be evaluated as $R \leq 11/37 =$

0.2973. Thus, if the sunk costs to enter will not be greater than ($R^c + 1 =$) 1.2973 times the

minimum sunk cost to enter, no price rise will occur. On the other hand, if $R > 1.2973$, a

---

[15] We choose N=5 to proxy the competitive conditions associated with the marginal antitrust case. The DOJ Guidelines view markets as "highly concentrated" if the relevant Herfindahl-Hirschman Index (HHI) is greater than 1800, which can be interpreted as 10000/1800=5.56 equal sized firms. This implies that a market with five equally sized firms (HHI=2000) creates a highly concentrated market structure, which if not offset by other market characteristics (such as the threat of entry or market characteristics that discourage collusion) may generate an anticompetitive effect. Uri and Coate (1987) point out, however, there is no empirical reason to believe that any particular cutoff level of market concentration such as 1800 is related to the likelihood of anticompetitive behavior.

cartel will find it *ex ante* profitable to risk the threat of new entry and will engage in limit pricing.

One issue that often arises in antitrust is whether economies of scale constitute an entry barrier. (See, for example, Scherer and Ross, 1989, at 424.) In the model here, N represents the inverse of economies of scale. If economies of scale are a barrier, $dR^c/dN < 0$. Differentiating (16) yields

(17)    $dR^c/dN = 2\lambda/[N+2\lambda(N+1)] - \lambda(2N+1)(1+2\lambda)/[N+2\lambda(N+1)]^2$.

A priori, (17) indicates that it is ambiguous whether economies of scale reduce the threat of entry. Increased economies of scale likely increase the costs of entering because such entry will have a larger impact on price. This larger impact on price, however, constitutes a greater threat to incumbents. Further, it increases the available level of payments from a buyer coalition. Evaluating (17) given N=5 implies that increasing economies of scale act to reduce the threat of entry if $\lambda < .5$.

### C. Growing Markets and Entry

We can adjust our model slightly to accommodate the dynamics of growing markets. Assume that before the game starts, but after incumbents have sunk their costs, the market grows by some factor g>0.[16] Demand for the industry's product now equals $(1+g)Q$. In this circumstance

(18a)  $^GP^I = (1+g)BQ+A$           (18b) $^G\pi^I = (1+g)^2Q^2B/2$

(19a)  $^GP^E = (1+g)KBQ+A$         (19b) $^G\pi^E = (1+g)^2Q^2BK/2$

---

[16] Note that growth in this context can mean either a positive shock to demand or a decrease in available supply due to depreciation.

(20) $\quad {}^G\pi^E_e = (1+g)^2 Q^2 KB/2(N+1)$

(21) $\quad {}^G\pi^E_i = (1+g)^2 Q^2 K^2 B/2.$

An entering firm will capture $((1+g)^2-1)Q^2KB/2(N+1)$ additional profits in infra-marginal rents. Further, the buyer coalition is now willing to pay an additional $\lambda((1+g)^2-1)(1-K)Q^2B$ to induce entry. Thus, entry becomes more profitable to the entrant and the buyer coalition in this scenario by $((1+g)^2-1)S_L$ and entry will occur no matter what the cartel does with probability $((1+g)^2-1)/R$. (We assume that $R>(1+g)^2-1$.)

Given this, the cartel will maximize its profits assuming that entry will not occur absent collusion. If entry does not occur absent collusion, the actual sunk costs of the most favorable entrant $S^E$ are distributed uniformly in the range $[(1+g)^2 S_L, (R+1)S_L]$. Thus, the probability of entry in response to a price rise is ${}^G\sigma(p_m) = p_m\lambda(1+g)Q/(R+1-(1+g)^2)S_L$. The cartel thus maximizes profits over $p_m$, given the probability of entry

(22) $\text{Max } \pi = {}^G\sigma(p_m){}^G\pi^E_i + (1-{}^G\sigma(p_m)){}^G\pi^C(p_m)$

where ${}^G\pi^C(p_m) = {}^G\pi^I + p_m(1+g)Q$. Taking derivatives and setting equal to zero yields

(23) $\lambda(1+g)^3 Q^3 K^2 B/2(R-(1+g)^2+1)S_L + (1+g)Q$

$\quad - 2\lambda p_m(1+g)Q^2/(R-(1+g)^2+1)S_L - \lambda(1+g)^3 Q^3 B/2(R-(1+g)^2+1)S_L = 0.$

Dividing (23) by $(1+g)Q$ and rearranging terms yields

(24) $p_m^* = [(R-(1+g)^2+1)S_L/2\lambda Q][1 - \lambda(1-K^2)(1+g)^2 Q^2 B/2[R-(1+g)^2+1]S_L].$

No price rise implies

13

(25)  $2(R-(1+g)^2+1)S_L \leq \lambda(1-K^2)(1+g)^2Q^2B$

$2(R-(1+g)^2+1)Q^2BKH \leq \lambda(1-K^2)(1+g)^2Q^2B.$

$(R-(1+g)^2+1) \leq (1+g)^2[\lambda(2N+1)/[N+2\lambda N+2\lambda]$

$R \leq (1+g)^2[\lambda(2N+1)/[N+2\lambda N+2\lambda] + (1+g)^2 - 1.$

Letting $N=5$, $\lambda=.2$, and $g=.05$ implies $R \leq 0.4303$. Thus, in this example an increase in the market demand by 5 percent yields a 44.7 percent increase in the range of entry costs that deters an anticompetitive price rise.[17]

### D. Costs of Collusion and Entry

The model can also be generalized to allow for positive costs of collusion. Along these lines, we assume that cartel coordination requires the firms to incur both fixed and price-related costs.

(26)  $C(p_m) = Z + dP_mQ$          $Z>0, 1>d>0.$

The initial expenditure $(Z)$ proxies the costs necessary to organize the cartel and the variable expenditure $(d)$ represents the costs of policing the agreement; a function of the monopoly profits at risk.[18]

Given these costs must be incurred to increase price regardless of whether entry occurs, the cartel's profit maximizing problem over $p_m$ becomes

---

[17] This model does not imply that "entry" cannot happen in a declining industry. In a declining industry, collusion may be defeated if fringe firms see a higher price and choose not to exit. In effect, "not exiting" becomes entry. See Coate and Kleit (Forthcoming, 1991).

[18] Lanning (1987 at 167) points out that the higher the collusive price, the higher the gains from cheating, therefore requiring higher expenditures by the cartel for enforcement purposes.

(27)     Max $\pi = \sigma(p_m)\pi^E_i + (1-\sigma(p_m))\pi^C(p_m) - (Z + dPmQ)$.

Again taking derivatives and equating to zero

(28)     $\lambda Q^3 K^2 B/2RS_L + Q - 2\lambda p_m Q^2/RS_L - \lambda Q^3 B/2RS_L - dQ = 0$.

Rearranging (28) generates a new equation for price

(29)     $p_m^* = [RS_L/2\lambda Q] [(1-d) - \lambda(1-K^2)Q^2 B/2RS_L]$.

The only difference between (29) and (13) is the use of the term (1-d) instead of 1. Thus, the remaining analysis is identical except for the additional of (1-d) on the left-hand side of the analysis. This implies that (15) can be written in the more general form of

(30)     $R \leq [\lambda(2N+1)/[(N+2\lambda(N+1))(1-d)]$.

Integrating both the costs of collusion and the growth model yields

(31)     $R \leq (1+g)^2[\lambda(2N+1)/[(N+2\lambda(N+1))(1-d)] + (1+g)^2 - 1$.

Retaining the assumptions that $N=5$, $\lambda =.2$, and defining $d=.2$ generates a value of R of .372. If growth is considered (i.e. as in equation (31) with a value of .05) the value is .512. This value is 72 percent higher than the initial value for a stagnant market with no costs of collusion.

Even if the threat of entry by itself will not deter a price increase, it is possible that the optimal price increase will be so small that the cartel is unable to cover the fixed costs of collusion. Thus, collusive activity will not occur, unless the firms can impose a sufficient price increase to cover the fixed costs of cartelization. This implies that the solution to (27) must be positive at the optimal price. Thus, as the fixed costs of collusion increase from zero, small price increases optimal under (28) generate a loss for the cartel, so no price increase will occur.

## IV.    Large Buyers in Recent Antitrust Cases

Empirical evidence on the threat of buyer-induced entry is inherently difficult to obtain, because it is the threat of entry, not entry itself, that defeats an anticompetitive price increase. It is possible, however, to gather evidence on the ability of buyer coalitions to induce entry by reviewing litigated cases where actual or potential buyer coalitions played a role. Perhaps the best example of a buyer coalition actually defeating anticompetitive pricing is described in *Sewell Plastics Inc. v. Coca Cola Co.* 720 F. Supp. 1186 (W.D.N.C. 1988), aff'd. 912 F.2d 463 (1990), cert. denied 1991. Sewell Plastics, one of the innovators of plastic soft drink bottles, attempted to maintain high prices into the 1980's (see *Sewell Plastics* 720 F. Supp. at 1207). In 1981, a group of Coca Cola bottlers approached Sewell and tried to negotiate lower prices by threatening entry. When Sewell failed to offer a sufficient discount, the bottlers created a joint venture to enter the market. (The District Court decision at 1208 indicates that such cooperatives are common in this industry.) The entrant, SouthEastern Container, grew to obtain a 33.5 percent share of the plastic bottle market and prices fell from $220 per thousand in 1982 to $146 in 1986 (see *id*. at 1210-1212). Thus, when induced by Sewell to actually enter, the bottlers succeeded at pushing price down dramatically.[19]

---

[19] Sewell's response to the successful entry was to sue in federal court alleging a litany of antitrust violations. After three years of pre-trial maneuvers, the defendants prevailed on a motion for summary judgement as the judge concluded that the plaintiff had raised no issue of material fact for a jury to decide even though 13 feet of paper (over three million pages of

Additional support for the idea of buyer-induced entry can be gleaned from examining the merger challenges litigated by the government since 1982 (see Table One).[20] A review of litigated cases presents examples of when courts believed that the threat of entry was sufficient to maintain competition or when parties induced actual entry to create competition at vertically-related levels of production.[21]

One of the first observations from reviewing recent merger cases is that it is relatively rare to have a merger litigated in Federal court involving direct sales to atomistic consumers. Even consumer goods can be sold through retailers that are large enough to create new entry. Other consumer goods are sold through mixed systems with some consumers purchasing directly and others through large buyer groups. The medical industry represents the most obvious example of this type of system. Finally, when atomistic consumers face monopolistic sellers in retailing, buyer coalition arguments can easily be inverted and applied to input suppliers. Thus, for almost any class of mergers, buyer strategy arguments, or their equivalent, can be entertained.

The simplest buyer coalition argument involves large buyers purchasing from a concentrated group of sellers. Examples from litigated cases include carbon black (a key input into tires), aircraft transparencies (a vital component of aircraft), and 25 mm second generation night vision tubes (the crucial input for a class of night vision devices used for

---

documents) was filed with the court. The court observed (at 1200-1) that "the volume of paper which a modern law firm can produce is often greater than a busy district judge can read and evaluate with care." For a discussion of the legal uncertainty with respect to buyer cooperatives, see Jacobson and Dorman (Forthcoming, 1991).

[20] For merger policy, June 14, 1982 is a watershed date, marking the revision of the merger guidelines. A further revision followed two years later, but most of the changes only clarified the 1982 guidelines. By limiting the merger sample to cases after June 14, 1982, we maximize the chances of finding decisions based on the improved economic model of competition in the 1982 and 1984 Guidelines.

[21] We note that our model implies that in some circumstances the threat of entry will deter a price increase, in others a price rise will be *ex ante* profitable but not *ex post* as it induces entry, and in others entry occurs solely due to market growth.

17

military purposes). Although the potential for buyer-induced entry in these examples appears clear, the relevant decisions imply that a buyer coalition would have had difficulty inducing entry, because entry was technically a long and difficult process. In other cases, entry appeared to be much easier. For example, in *U.S. v. County Lake et al.* (1990 at 11) District Court Judge Renner found that the large milk distributors, who controlled over 90 percent of the market, could and would seek suppliers outside the local area or vertically integrate in response to anticompetitive pricing by local milk processors. This was considered sufficient to maintain competition. Similarly, in *U.S. v. Calmar* (1985 at 1304), District Court Judge Debevoise found that buyers of pump dispensers and sprayers would react to an anticompetitive price increases by either vertically integrating or entering into a joint venture with another firm to make such products.

Another example of the potential for buyer strategies can be found in the recent *Baker Hughes* decision.[22] District Court Judge Gesell noted the major customers for hardrock hydraulic mining equipment would insist on receiving competitive bids and were likely to have contacts with mining equipment manufacturers in Canada (see *Baker Hughes* 731 F. Supp. at 10-11). Thus, Judge Gesell felt that buyer strategies would facilitate successful entry into the U.S. market were the merger to induce collusion. A key point in the decision appears to be the sophistication of buyers rather than their absolute size. Thus, even when the buyers do not have large market shares, it has been concluded that they may be able to contribute to maintaining competition. Similarly in *Echlin Manufacturing Co.*, 105 F.T.C. 410 (1985), firms (resellers) that purchased carburetor kits from assemblers were observed to have some power to maintain competitive prices. Moreover, the Commission noted that resellers could either have another firm package the carburetor kits for them or

---

[22] *Baker Hughes*, supra note 3.

do it themselves (*Echlin* at 467). Thus, buyers were considered potential entrants whose existence was believed to keep the market competitive.

While buyer-induced entry has had significant success as a defense tactic in merger litigations, it by no means represents a panacea for defendants. For instance, buyer strategy arguments have been given little weight in hospital merger decisions where third party payers (Blue Cross and the government) appear to be very large buyers.[23] In *Hospital Corp. of Am. v. F.T.C.*, 106 F.T.C 361, 509 (1985), 807 F.2d 1381 (7th Cir. 1986), cert. denied 107 S.Ct. 1975 (1987), the Commission rejected the buyer strategy argument, observing Blue Cross could not switch its business to hospitals outside the geographic market. In reviewing the case, Judge Posner developed this idea further by noting third party payers are not completely analogous to large buyers (*Hospital Corp. of Am.* 807 F 2d at 1391). Insurance companies are obligated to pay the contracted portion of the medical charges for their customers as opposed to large buyers that could strategically reduce purchases of product. It is not clear how the third party payer could threaten to move large amounts of business away from the oligopolists, although conceivably they could help to develop HMOs. Likewise, in *U.S. v. Rockford Memorial Corp.*, 898 F.2d 1278 1285 (7th Cir. 1990), Judge Posner (at 1285) observed that the third party issue affected the elasticity of demand, but the overall effect on competition was unclear. We can note that both hospital cases involved relatively large barriers to entry (such as certificate of need regulation), with no potential entrant apparently being "close" to entering. Thus, the third party payers were unlikely to defeat the price increase by motivating new entrants to come into the market. In *U.S. v. Carillon Health Systems*, 707 F. Supp 840, 849 (W.D. Vir. 1989), however, the court held the ability of other hospitals to expand was sufficient to outweigh the concerns caused by the

---

[23] A simplistic argument might note that Medicare and Medicaid set price for hospitals, so even a monopolist could not raise price. In addition to ignoring the potential for price increases to nongovernment patients, the assumption that government pricing is exogenous ignores the potential for hospitals to manipulate the system to their advantage.

increased concentration level. Although the concept of buyer induced-entry was not explicitly mentioned in this decision, it could have easily been integrated into the analysis. Overall, buyer strategy arguments may be applied to hospital mergers, but only in limited fact situations.

Finally, the idea of buyer-induced entry can easily be inverted into supplier strategy arguments. If a retailer attempts to monopolize a geographic area, both suppliers and consumers may suffer injury. The supplier can respond by inducing entry to defeat the anticompetitive overcharge. An example of this behavior comes from the movie theater industry. In *U.S. v. Syufy Enterprises*, 712 F. Supp. (N.D. Cal. 1989), aff'd 903 F.2d 659 (9th Cir. 1990), the court decisions report that Orion Releasing Group shifted its business to a small second run theater after a contract dispute with defendant Syufy. This action meant that a new competitor entered the first run market in Las Vegas which businessman Raymond Syufy had acquired a (short-run) market share of over 90 percent. District Court Judge Orrick and Judge Kozinski for the Appeals Court chronicled the success of the entrant and both concluded that Syufy's various movie theater mergers in Las Vegas had no anticompetitive effect. Judge Kozinski concluded:

> More fundamentally, in a free economy the market itself imposes a tough enough discipline on all market actors, large and small. Every supplier of goods and services is integrated into an endless chain of supply and demand relationships, making it dependent on the efficiency and goodwill of upstream suppliers as well as the patronage of customers. Absent structural constraints that keep competition from performing its levelling function, few businesses can dictate terms to customers or suppliers with impunity. It's risky business even to try. As Syufy learned in dealing with Orion and his other suppliers, a large company is often more vulnerable to a squeeze play than a smaller one. It is for that reason that neither size nor market share lone suffice to establish a monopoly. Without the power to exclude competition, large companies that try to throw their weight around may find

20

themselves sitting ducks for leaner, hungrier competitors. Or, as Syufy saw, the tactic may boomerang, causing big trouble with suppliers.[24]


## V. Conclusion

This paper attempts to bridge the gap between judicial decisions and economic theory relating to entry. Our model shows how buyer strategies can be used, at least in some circumstances, to overcome the presence of sunk costs such that the threat of entry is able to deter price increases. Such threats are likely to be most effective when sophisticated buyers (sellers) make up a large portion of the relevant output (input) market and when the lowest cost potential entrant is relatively "close" to entering the market absent an anticompetitive price increase. One, though not the only way, of thinking of this concept is asking how near to contestability a particular market is. Our model also implies that antitrust law should be more lenient towards joint ventures in vertically related markets to allow a wider array of buyer strategies. Recent court decisions clearly show that the judiciary recognizes many of these concepts. This paper is an attempt to present this phenomena to economists, as well as to allow jurists to give more formal structure to their decisions.

---

[24] *Syufy*, 903 F.2d at 671. Judge Kozinski allegedly mentioned over 200 movie titles in his opinion. We found 4 in this quote.

## Bibliography

Baker, Jonathan B., "Identifying Cartel Policing Under Uncertainty: The U.S. Steel Industry, 1933-1939," Journal of Law and Economics 32 (1989) S47-S76.

Baumol, William J., Panzar, John C. Jr., and Willig, Robert D., Contestable Markets and the Theory of Industry Structure, Harcourt Brace Jovanovich, New York (1982).

Caves, Richard, and Porter, Robert, "Market Structure, Oligopoly, and Stability of Market Shares," Journal of Industrial Economics 26 (1978).

Coate, Malcolm B., and Kleit, Andrew N., "Antitrust Policy for Declining Industries," Journal of Institutional and Theoretical Economics, Forthcoming 147 (1991).

Crawford, Vincent P. and Sobel, Joel, "Strategic Information Transmission," Econometrica 50 (1982) 1431-1451.

Demsetz, Harold, "Why Regulate Utilities?", Journal of Law and Economics 11 (1968) 55-65.

Gelman, Judith R., and Salop, Steven C., "Judo Economics: Capacity Limitation and Coupon Competition," Rand Journal of Economics 14 (1983) 315-323.

Harrington, Joseph E., Jr., "Collusion and Predation Under (Almost) Free Entry," International Journal of Industrial Organization 7 (1989) 381-401.

Jacobson, Jonathan M., and Dorman, Gary J., "Joint Purchasing, Monopsony, and Antitrust," Antitrust Bulletin 36 (Forthcoming, 1991).

Lanning, Steven G., "Costs of Maintaining a Cartel," Journal of Industrial Economics 36 (December 1987) 157-174.

McAfee, R. Preston, and McMillan, John, "Auctions and Bidding," Journal of Economic Literature, 25 (1987) 699-738.

Scheffman, David T., and Spiller, Pablo, T., "Buyers and Entry Barriers," Federal Trade Commission Working Paper No. 154 (August 1987).

Scherer, F.M. and Ross, David, Industrial Market Structure and Economics Performance, Houghlin Mifflin Company, Boston (3rd edition, 1989)

Schmalansee, Richard, "Ease of Entry: Has the Concept Been Applied Too Readily?", Antitrust Law Journal 56:1 (1987) 41-51.

Sexton, Richard J., and Sexton, Terri A., "Cooperatives as Entrants," Rand Journal of Economics 18:4 (1987) 581-596.

Stiglitz, Joseph E., "Do Entry Conditions Vary Across Markets?", in Brookings Papers on Economic Activity (Microeconomics) (Martin Neil Bailey and Clifford Winston, ed.) 3 (1987) 883-947.

U.S. Department of Justice, "Merger Guidelines," <u>Antitrust and Trade Regulation Report</u>, No. 1169, Special Supplement (June 14, 1984).

Uri, Noel and Coate, Malcolm B., "The Department of Justice Merger Guidelines: The Search for Empirical Support," <u>International Review of Law and Economics</u>, 7 (June 1987) 113-120.

Yu, Ben T., "Potential Competition and Contracting For Innovation," <u>Journal of Law and Economics</u> 24 (1981) 215-238.

Table One

Products in Merger Challenges

Government Cases in Federal Court, 1982-1990

(Number of Cases in Parentheses)

| | |
|---|---|
| Banking Services (2) | Gasoline Distribution |
| Carbon Black for Tires | Rigid Wall Containers |
| Pre-recorded Music | Industrial Dry Corn |
| Commercial Trash Collection | Automatic Railroad Tampers |
| Carburetor Kits | Supermarkets |
| Corrugating Medium | Night Vision Tubes |
| Sprayers and Dispensers | First Run Movie Releases |
| Milling of Paddy Rice | Fluid Milk |
| Plastic Fuel Stocks (2) | Hardrock Hydraulic Mining Equipment |
| Carbonated Soft Drinks | Printing Services |
| Aircraft Transparencies | Schmidt-Cassegrain Telescopes |
| Hospital Services (3) | Movie Laboratory Service Agreements |

Source: Various Federal Court Merger Decisions